The

Heartbreak

Bind:

Recovering from Heartbreak and Rediscovering Resilience

By

ROBERT T. BARNER

TABLE OF CONTENT

INTRODUCTION

ANALYZING THE HEARTBREAK BIND

Heartbreak, that mysterious yet ubiquitous feeling, is a complex emotional tapestry with the capacity to fundamentally change who we are. We reluctantly embarked on this journey, often caught off guard when a bond we thought would last forever broke. By exploring the depths of this emotional storm, "The Heartbreak Bind: Recovering When the One You Love Deeply Takes the Worst Toll on You" seeks to guide you through the difficult path of healing, self-discovery, and escape from the bindings of sadness.

Before we embark on this journey, we must first make sense of the complexity of the emotional labyrinth that is sadness.

It is a symphony of emotions, maybe the most subdued of them being desire. Feelings such as anger, despair, loss, and confusion are also experienced.

The emotional landscape is broad and varied, a complex web capable of entangling the most resilient souls. This chapter explores the nuances of pain, busting stereotypes and generalizations to show the true complexity of the human heart during bereavement. Generally speaking, heartbreak is connected to depressing music, shattered promises, and weeping faces. Under these clichés, however, lies a more profound truth. Heartbreak is a complicated emotion since it affects every individual and relationship differently. It's a personal journey that calls for acknowledgement, acceptance, and understanding; not everyone will find it appealing. This chapter aims to reframe suffering by asking readers to consider its complexities, nuances, and transformative power.

Recognizing Trends and Warning Signs

Breakups are commonplace in the dynamic realm of relationships. Before they happen, warning signs like unspoken tensions, dissatisfied murmurs, and little tremors in the basis of a relationship are often evident. In Chapter 2, we look at these causes and the mechanisms that lead to the breakdown of relationships.

By recognizing these warning signs, readers may get a deeper understanding of the complexities of human connection and better equip themselves to deal with the challenges that precede loss.

The grief tightens as we sail over the rough waters of a failing relationship. The emotional toll is most apparent at these times. Even when a relationship ends, identity loss, unfulfilled expectations, and a profound sense of rejection may leave long-lasting scars. Chapter 2 goes into great detail on the emotional toll that grief has on us and how it impacts our ability to go on and define who we are.

Grief Stages and Techniques for Coping

After a relationship ends, grief becomes an unavoidable traveling companion on the route through sadness. In Chapter 3, we go through the stages of grief and acknowledge the intense emotions that accompany each step.

The coping mechanisms that help readers navigate the emotional rollercoaster—from denial to acceptance—are outlined.

By understanding the complexity of mourning, people may begin the healing process and find solace in the midst of emotional turmoil.

Building Resilience and Regaining Self-Belief

Chapter 4 is all about the hard job of rebuilding trust, especially with oneself. Once destroyed, confidence may feel like a distant memory. However, it's a necessary place to start as the healing process begins. This chapter offers practical exercises that support individuals in rediscovering their inner resilience and strength, which are essential components of conquering grief. By finding inner strength, readers may open the door to self-discovery and a reinvigorated sense of purpose.

Ideas for Growing Oneself and Moving Forward

The story's emphasis shifts to the lessons learned and the potential for personal growth as the last chapters approach.

In Chapter 5, We challenges readers to think about the transformative power of grief and makes significant deductions and discoveries that might have an impact on future relationships and personal development.

This chapter celebrates perseverance and acknowledges the power that emerges from the crucible of grief.

We summarize the key insights from each chapter in the conclusion to provide a thorough understanding that might be helpful to those who are experiencing sorrow. We wrap up with some parting thoughts of wisdom, emphasizing how important it is to approach the healing process with courage and optimism. It provides an overview of the subject and a guide for readers to follow as they set out to break free from the shackles of sadness.

This is not just a book; The Heartbreak Bind is a companion for anybody navigating the choppy seas of sadness.

Within its pages, readers will find solace, compassion, and practical guidance as they rewrite their tales, navigate the emotional labyrinth, and emerge from it stronger than before. Beyond only overcoming grief, this journey is about rediscovering your inner resilience, opening doors for personal growth, and embracing the limitless opportunities that await on the other side of the heartache.

CHAPTER 1

THE ANATOMY OF HEARTBREAK

Heartbreak is a complicated and sophisticated emotional experience that includes a wide range of thoughts, emotions, and bodily sensations. It is the tremendous sadness and grief that result from the disintegration of a strong emotional relationship or a substantial loss at its heart.

The anatomy of sorrow starts with the first shock, a piercing anguish that often presents in the chest. This experience is not only metaphorical; studies show that emotional pain engages the same brain pathways as physical pain, emphasizing the physicality of grief.

The mind becomes a battlefield of opposing feelings as emotional traumas grow.

The phases of grieving, which include denial, anger, bargaining, sadness, and acceptance, play out in a chaotic dance. The mind struggles with the breakdown of expectations and the harsh reality of a broken connection.

Concurrently, the heart experiences dramatic alterations. Emotional ups and downs may appear physically, creating irregular heartbeats, weariness, and even pain. Once a sign of love and connection, the heart has become a visceral reminder of the suffering felt.

Heartbreak's anatomy goes beyond the person, impacting social relationships and everyday life. In the aftermath, relationships with friends, family, and oneself are altered. The environment, which was previously alive with shared experiences and laughter, may look desaturated and alien.

Nonetheless, there is a tremendous chance for development within the ruins. The healing process starts as time passes. Scars may persist, but they serve as a reminder of tenacity and endurance.

Though painful, the anatomy of grief eventually adds to the rich fabric of human experience, encouraging empathy, self-discovery, and the fortitude to love again.

What Is Heartbreak?

Heartbreak is a heavy word that conjures up images of cracked photographs, depressing background music, and individuals with tears running down their faces.

These platitudes hardly begin to convey the profound complexity of mourning, despite the fact that they are founded on genuine emotions. To understand and cope with grief in a healthy way, we must reframe what it means to recover from it.

In essence, heartbreak is a significant bodily response to the loss of a deep emotional bond. Two souls are bound together by the unraveling of intricate threads that leave a path of memories, emotions, and unfulfilled expectations in their wake. Beyond the corny sentiments lie a range of emotions, from the searing anguish of an unexpected loss to the profound, never-ending ache of longing.

This chapter peels back the superficial layers of popular thought to question the oversimplified narratives that often mold our understanding of grief. No two heartbreaks are the same; each has its own set of emotions, events, and aftermath.

By delving into the subtleties of the emotional landscape, we want to help readers embrace the singularity of their grief experiences.

We looked into the question: What does each of us really mean when we experience heartbreak? It's a route that calls for introspection and the willingness to confront the raw, sometimes painful emotions that accompany terminating a significant relationship. People may begin to dispel any myths that could be preventing them from healing by realizing how complicated loss is.

The first step in the process is realizing that heartbreak is about more than simply a romantic relationship ending. Its claws pierce relationships with friends, family, and even the dissolution of commercial partnerships.

Each context adds nuance to the incident, affecting how the emotions respond and heal.

Few threads in the enormous fabric of human emotions are as delicate, poignant, and resonant as those woven by the complicated dance of grief. It is a story that transcends time and space, leaving its imprint on the collective human experience. Heartbreak is a deep and universal tune that has echoed through the years, spoken in the solitary regions where hearts battle with the complexity of broken love.

Heartbreak is, at its core, an unfathomable anguish, an emotional rift that rips through the very fabric of our being. It arises not simply from the breakdown of sexual relationships but also from broken friendship links, shattered family ties, and the unraveling of connections that previously characterized our feeling of belonging. It is an emotional crucible in which our most sensitive portions are exposed to the biting winds of loss.

When love turns to sadness, a delicate ballet of emotions takes place.

The first shock, a symphony of sadness, and the lingering remnants of what was—all of these pieces come together to form a mosaic of sorrow and contemplation. Heartbreak is intertwined with rage, grief, perplexity, and a terrible feeling of emptiness. As we read this book, we will travel the maze of emotions that is sorrow, unraveling the complexity with empathy and understanding.

The metaphor of unwinding threads transforms into a painful prism through which we experience grief.

These threads are more than just links; they constitute the foundation of our emotional lives. They tie us together via shared experiences, dreams, and connected futures. When tragedy comes, however, these strands rip and unravel, leaving behind a strewn tapestry. Our journey will be an examination of each strand and each feeling as we strive to comprehend, disentangle, and eventually create a new healing story.

Heartbreak is a universal emotion that cuts beyond cultural, historical, and geographic barriers. It's a symphony of grief performed on the strings of the human heart.

This book acknowledges the universality of sorrow while still acknowledging the distinctive subtleties that distinguish each experience. The strands of loss connect us together on the common path of human vulnerability, whether it's the silent tears shed in isolation or the shared experiences of recovery.

While loss may seem to be an unstoppable force, this story is one of perseverance and the human spirit's ability to heal. We will travel the journey to recovery, investigating how people find themselves after experiencing tragedy.

From self-reflection to emotional resilience rebuilding, each step is a step toward a new chapter, a story of regeneration ready to be written.

Let this book be a companion in the areas where emotions are raw and healing is a slow unfolding as we start on this path of unraveling the threads of grief. The next chapters will walk us through the difficulties of spotting warning signals, traversing the mourning spectrum, and eventually finding ourselves in the aftermath of tragedy.

Each phrase is a thread in the fabric of compassion, understanding, and the prospect of a better daybreak after the darkest night.

As we redefine grief, we encourage readers to think about their own interpretations and points of view. What does heartbreak mean to you? How has it shown itself in your life? By acknowledging the diversity of experiences, readers may start to loosen the emotional bonds that often bind individuals to societal standards, facilitating a more authentic and individual healing process.

We also look at the physical aspects of heartache. Science suggests that leaving a significant relationship might put your body in a stressful state, just as it does when you're physically hurt. Knowledge about these physiological reactions confirms that sadness has a major impact on one's physical and mental well-being, contributing to a more thorough knowledge of the phenomenon.

By the end of this chapter, readers will have a more nuanced perspective on grief, one that transcends clichés and embraces the complete gamut of emotions that accompany this complex human experience.

People are more equipped to manage the next chapters, which go into further depth on the intricacies of the grieving process, now that they have this understanding.

We refuse to accept the clichés that romanticize or oversimplify this nuanced emotional hurt; therefore, we will continue to reinvent grief. Though dramatic gestures and sorrowful scenes are often used in movies to depict heartbreak, the actual world is significantly more nuanced.

To get a better grasp of the anatomy of heartbreak, we look at the many ways that it manifests itself in the human mind. It's not only about someone leaving our lives; it's also about not planning forward, not having a shared future, and having to reevaluate your identity in the absence of a significant other.

Heartbreak may trigger an existential crisis that compels the sufferer to reflect on their own worth, meaning of relationships, and purpose in life.

Heartbreak encompasses a complex interplay of conflicting feelings and a broad spectrum of emotions, such as anger, remorse, and sadness. It involves not only grieving for a person's passing but also losing routines, goals, and the little things in life that sum up to a relationship.

Acknowledging this intricate emotional landscape is crucial to the recovery process.

Particularized Knowledge:

Each grief is unique, shaped by the individuals involved, their histories, and the environment in which their connection exists. Breaking up might be liberating for many individuals, but it can also be quite painful. In this study, we accept that there isn't a single, universally applicable approach to healing and instead value the diversity of grief experiences.

Rejecting societal conventions and schedules that dictate predetermined grief and healing processes is crucial.

There is no typical to-do list for moving on or a predetermined amount of time for healing. People may free themselves from the urge to fit into set timelines and storylines by recognizing and respecting the individuality of every loss.

Effects on Cognition and Psychology

1.   Cognitive Fog and Difficulties in Making Decisions: Heartbreak is not limited to the emotional sphere; it also permeates the cognitive sphere, obscuring reasoning.

 In the wake of heartbreak, people frequently struggle with mental confusion, finding even the most basic tasks difficult to complete and routine decisions difficult to make.

This emotional turbulence's byproduct, cognitive fog, can exacerbate feelings of vulnerability and disorientation.

In the depths of heartbreak, decision-making—which is normally a routine part of daily life—becomes an impossible undertaking. It becomes more difficult to consider options, foresee outcomes, and make wise decisions.

This section examines the difficulties people encounter when heartbreak clouds their cognitive faculties, highlighting the significance of patience and self-compassion during this time of cognitive vulnerability.

2. Psychological Correspondence: Heartbreak leaves a psychological mark, a resonance that reverberates through mental corridors long after the initial shock has worn off. This is in addition to the immediate emotional turmoil. Heartbreak leaves scars that appear in many different psychological domains and affect attitudes, perceptions, and interactions in the future.

A weakened sense of self-worth is one of the long-lasting psychological effects. A person's self-esteem can be completely destroyed by heartbreak, which makes them doubt their worth and desirability.

This chapter explores techniques for reestablishing a positive sense of self after heartbreak and examines the complex ways in which heartbreak shapes one's perception of oneself.

Another psychological afterglow of heartbreak is trust issues. A deep sense of skepticism brought on by betrayal or loss during a breakup can make it difficult to trust people, including oneself, at times. This section walks readers through the delicate process of reestablishing trust in interpersonal relationships as well as in one's own sense of judgment and intuition.

Furthermore, heartbreak can set off a chain reaction of bothersome memories and thoughts that play back old scenes like an endless movie reel. Rumination is a psychological phenomenon that can obstruct the healing process.

Techniques for controlling bothersome thoughts and refocusing cognitive attention on positive aspects of life are discussed, enabling people to take back control of their mental environments.

This chapter seeks to shed light on the long-lasting effects of heartbreak, beyond the momentary emotional turmoil, by dissecting the cognitive and psychological effects of heartbreak. Gaining an understanding of these subtleties is essential to holistic healing, as it promotes resilience in the complex mental domains as well as the emotional realm.

The Emotional Impact of Heartbreak on Mental Health

Heartbreak can have a profound and long-lasting impact on one's mental health. The emotional toll of a broken heart can be severe and manifest in a variety of ways. Individuals experiencing heartbreak may feel profound sadness, despair, and a sense of loss. The pain can be both emotional and physical, with symptoms such as insomnia, appetite changes, and general lethargy.

One of the most difficult aspects of heartbreak is the effect it has on one's self-esteem and self-worth.

Rejection and the end of a significant relationship can cause feelings of inadequacy, abandonment, and self-doubt.

This can exacerbate the emotional distress by contributing to a negative cycle of self-talk and self-doubt.

Each person's grieving process is unique, but it frequently includes stages of denial, anger, bargaining, depression, and acceptance.

Moving through these stages takes time, and the length of healing differs from person to person. Individuals must give themselves the time and space they need to navigate their emotions and seek help from friends, family, or mental health professionals.

In some cases, heartbreak can precipitate or worsen mental health conditions like depression or anxiety. Individuals must be aware of their mental health during this difficult time and seek professional help if necessary. Therapy and counseling can provide a safe space for people to process their emotions, develop coping strategies, and rebuild their sense of self.

In the aftermath of heartbreak, self-care becomes critical. Engaging in enjoyable activities, maintaining a healthy routine, and fostering social connections can all help with the healing process. Individuals must also challenge negative thought patterns and work to cultivate a positive and compassionate relationship with themselves.

Finally, healing from heartbreak is a slow process that necessitates patience and self-compassion.

While intense emotions are normal, seeking professional help and taking proactive steps toward self-care can help with mental and emotional well-being in the aftermath of heartbreak.

Heartbreak can cause psychological shock, which is a very real condition. Heartbreak, like any other trauma, can cause psychological shock, also known as "emotional shock" or "acute stress reaction." And emotional shock causes more than just anxiety, fear, and a sense of disbelief.

Physical Impact on Health

1.   Hormone and Stress:

After a breakup, stress becomes an unwanted associate. The emotional upheaval sets off the body's stress response, which releases a burst of cortisol, a hormone closely related to stress regulation. Short-term stress responses require cortisol, but sustained elevation can cause a number of health problems. These might include poor immune system performance, disturbed sleep, and increased vulnerability to sickness.

This section explores the complex relationship between cortisol levels and emotional stress and how they affect the body's overall balance.

2. Emotional Unrest and Sleep Disturbances:

One significant component of the physical toll of heartbreak is the mutually beneficial relationship between emotional turmoil and sleep disturbances. Night sweats, insomnia, and restless nights are common side effects of a turbulent emotional journey.

This section of the chapter looks at how sleep disturbances can lead to a vicious cycle of vulnerability and exhaustion, in addition to making emotional difficulties worse. During a breakup, techniques for promoting improved sleep hygiene and regaining peaceful nights become essential parts of comprehensive care.

3. Vulnerability and the Immune Response:

Even though the immune system protects the body from outside threats, heartbreak still has an impact on it.

Prolonged stress, often associated with heartache, can weaken the immune system, making people more vulnerable to infections and diseases. Here, we examine the delicate relationship between immune function and emotional stability, emphasizing the value of supporting the body's natural defenses when vulnerability is at its highest. Holistic healing incorporates immune-supporting techniques like stress management, physical activity, and diet.

4.   Integrative Medicine and Self-Compassion:

Adopting holistic care is sparked by realizing the physical effects of heartache.

This entails adopting habits that support general health and realizing the connection between emotional and physical well-being. Key components of holistic care include balanced nutrition, mindful breathing, and light physical activity. Furthermore, self-compassion takes center stage, recognizing that during the healing process, taking care of one's physical needs is not only a practical necessity but also a critical act of self-love.

As the physical aspects of heartbreak are revealed, people become more cognizant of the complex relationship that exists between emotional distress and physical reactions. This knowledge forms the cornerstone for putting into practice deliberate tactics that promote holistic well-being, enabling people to walk the healing journey with fortitude, self-care, and a revitalized sense of energy.

The Way Forward

We want readers to reflect on their own definitions and experiences of the emotion. Which characteristics of heartbreak fit you personally? In what ways has your specific experience conformed to or deviated from societal norms?

The foundation for the next chapters, which go further into the nuances of grieving recovery, is laid in this chapter.

In the next chapters, we'll look at the mechanics of relationships, how to avoid the warning signals of approaching sadness, and the psychological effects of heartbreak. With a thorough understanding of the anatomy of heartbreak, readers will be prepared to embark on a journey of self-discovery, healing, and liberation from the constraints that bind them after a major emotional loss.

CHAPTER 2

THE RELATIONSHIP'S UNRAVELING AND THE EMOTIONAL COST

Identifying Warning Signals and Patterns

Knowing the warning signals and the underlying dynamics in the maze of relationships is like having a compass that leads you through the turns and turns. The purpose of this section is to help readers become acutely aware of the little changes that might indicate relationship problems. It explores the subtler components, such as subtle changes in communication patterns, a decline in emotional closeness, and unsaid tensions, rather than focusing on the more overt indicators, such as furious fights or open conflicts. Early detection of these warning indicators provides people with a priceless chance to deal with problems head-on and promotes open dialogue and understanding.

It's a proactive strategy for preserving relationships, highlighting how crucial it is to continue to feel the connection's emotional pulse. The intention is to give people the tools they need to handle the intricacies of relationships with better awareness and resilience, not to induce dread or worry.

Being able to see warning signals and understand the underlying dynamics in the fragile ecology of relationships is like having an emotional radar that is well calibrated. It's an art that requires not only watching outward actions but also having an innate understanding of the unspoken nuances—the minute changes in energy, the words that are not stated, the silent emotions that convey a great deal. We walk readers through the many facets of emotional intelligence in this investigation, offering a road map for negotiating the challenges of interpersonal relationships.

1. Communication Breakdown: Communication is the lifeblood of each relationship, and the health of the connection may be inferred from its patterns. There may be indicators of underlying problems, such as a gradual decrease in meaningful talks, a lack of shared humor, or a rise in the number of misunderstandings.

In order to promote open communication and handle issues before they become more serious, this section urges readers to pay attention to these tendencies.

2. Relationships are held together by emotional closeness, so when it wanes, it may be a cause for concern. This section of the chapter invites readers to consider how emotionally intimate their relationships are. Do spouses still confide in one another? Do they recognize the emotional needs of one another? People may take proactive measures to reestablish connection and strengthen the emotional ties that underpin a good relationship by identifying changes in emotional closeness.

3. Power Dynamics: Power dynamics affect relationships too, and keeping things in balance requires being able to identify imbalances. Readers are encouraged to investigate if there is an equitable allocation of power, whether both spouses feel heard and respected, and whether decision-making procedures are shared.

People may establish a relationship in which there is room for development on both sides and where each person's opinion is valued by resolving power disparities.

4.   Shared Responsibilities: In a partnership, responsibilities go beyond the personal to include day-to-day tasks and activities. Identifying warning indicators entails determining whether domestic and external obligations are distributed fairly. The relationship may suffer if one person feels overburdened or ignored when it comes to assigned responsibilitics. In order to ensure that both parties contribute to the success of the relationship, this investigation promotes an open discussion about expectations.

It takes a combination of introspection and sympathetic observation to comprehend these relationships. It involves developing an awareness that reaches under the surface to explore the relational and emotional currents that define the relationship.

People may empower themselves to direct the relationship toward a better trajectory or make educated judgments about its future by identifying warning flags early on and comprehending the nuances of these relationships.

This section essentially functions as a manual for cultivating heightened awareness—an emotional toolbox that enables people to address relationship problems with understanding, compassion, and a proactive stance toward preserving their emotional health.

The Breakdown of Relationships

When a relationship is breaking down, it usually happens gradually and is characterized by a sequence of seemingly unimportant events. This section of the chapter takes readers on an insightful trip across the emotional terrain of relationships that are on the verge of disintegration. It examines the fine dance between optimism and despair as people struggle to accept that the foundation, they previously believed to be firm is beginning to show symptoms of deterioration.

This investigation challenges readers to face the uncomfortable but necessary truth that uncertainty exists in relationships. It's a call to consider the emotional upheaval that comes before heartache, realizing that facing the emotional cost of the unraveling is the first step on the road to recovery.

The unraveling of a relationship is a complicated tapestry of emotions, experiences, and realizations that lay beyond the easily identifiable markers of its health.

In this part, readers are invited to travel across the emotional terrain of relationships that are about to collapse—a moving experience characterized by self-discovery, uncertainty, and the interaction of painful recognition and love.

1. Getting Through the Maze of Doubt: The road to heartache is often covered with doubt, causing the relationship's once-obvious road map to become hazy and unclear. It is a moment when people struggle with the dichotomy of holding on to what is left of love while realizing that change is inevitable. Hope and despair coexist throughout this time.

This section of the chapter offers readers guidance through this emotional maze and insights into the emotional rollercoaster that this stage is known for.

Acknowledging uncertainty gives people the confidence to ask tough questions. Is there a future that everyone agrees upon? Are the two partners developing together, or is the partnership starting to impede personal growth? Establishing the foundation for a more deliberate and thoughtful approach to the developing relationship, navigating this uncertainty calls for a careful balancing act between self-reflection and candid communication.

2.   Embracing the Reality of Emotions: When a relationship breaks down, it's a clash of feelings between the love that brought two people together and the sad truth that their circumstances have changed. This section of the chapter explores the emotional turbulence that accompanies this process and invites readers to face the unfiltered, sometimes contradictory feelings that surface.

It's about expressing the sorrow of losing a shared dream in addition to a spouse. There is no denying the intense agony, and this part offers readers comfort and understanding as they move from denial to acceptance throughout the grieving process. Through acknowledging and addressing these feelings, people establish the groundwork for recovery and development.

3.   Thoughts on the Development of the Relationship: When a relationship starts to fall apart, one must consider how it has progressed from the first spark of connection to the complexity that now defines it. Introspection is encouraged in this section as readers consider their own pivotal moments, missed cues, and changing needs as a couple.

People may get important insights into the dynamics of a relationship and make better judgments about its future by thinking back on the partnership's development.

In addition to fostering a greater awareness of one's own wants and aspirations, this introspective process lays the foundation for strengthening one's sense of self following the unraveling.

Essentially, this section of the chapter serves as a kind guide through the turbulent emotional period that comes before sorrow.

It recognizes the intricacy of feelings, gives people the tools they need to face uncertainty head-on, and lays the groundwork for the next chapters, which concentrate on grieving, healing, and the road to reconstruction.

Identity Loss in Relationships

The loss of identity is one of the most significant emotional costs of a failing relationship. Relationships have the power to change us; they shape our self-perception and help shape our developing sense of self. This part explores the psychological effects of losing one's identity and challenges readers to think about how their story about themselves could become mixed up with the relationship's narrative.

Consider a relationship as two pieces of a jigsaw that fit together to form a new image. Over time, you begin to share aspects of yourself and your experiences.

Being close to someone causes this natural melding to occur. It may, however, seem as if you're losing a piece of yourself as the relationship begins to fall apart.

1.   Combining identities: Picture yourself and your significant other taking pleasure in common interests, planning activities, and writing stories together. In intimate partnerships, this mixing of identities is commonplace. However, it's critical to acknowledge how much of your identity became entwined with the relationship when things started to go wrong. Are you putting less emphasis on your own interests? Do you have a feeling of loss when you consider your own aspirations and goals? The first step to taking back your identity is realizing this merging process.

2.   Adrift in the Aftermath: When a relationship breaks down, it's normal to feel disoriented and unanchored. There may be questions regarding your identity outside of the partnership. The breakup alters your goals, habits, and plans for the future. It's important to acknowledge this sense of being lost.

It all comes down to embracing the unknown and allowing yourself some alone time to consider your identity. This is a procedure that is essential to the healing process.

3.   Rebuilding a Sense of Self: Rebuilding oneself after a breakup is comparable to piecing together a storm-damaged structure. This section of the chapter provides helpful guidance. It inspires you to accept your uniqueness, develop new objectives, and rediscover what brings you joy. It's important to integrate the lessons acquired and develop into a stronger, more self-aware individual, rather than forgetting the common past.

Simply put, feeling as if a piece of yourself is missing after a breakup since so much of who you are now is connected to the relationship is what it means to lose your identity. Healing after a breakup requires realizing this, accepting the sensation of being lost, and then taking action to rebuild and rediscover who you are.

Readers are taken through the process of separating their sense of self from the relationship as the book explores the nuances of identity loss.

It promotes reflection on the ways in which people could have unintentionally combined their identities with those of their partners and provides guidance on how to reassemble an autonomous, strong, and self-empowered sense of self.

This section of the chapter is essentially a sympathetic examination of the emotional difficulties that arise when partnerships fall apart.

It opens the door to a deeper comprehension of the psychological toll that comes before sorrow by acknowledging the enormous influence on one's mental state.

Expanding upon these subheadings provides readers with a more sophisticated understanding of the dynamics and emotional terrain of dynamic partnerships. The goal is to provide a thorough framework that encourages self-awareness and gives people the ability to successfully negotiate the challenging journey toward healing and recovery.

Dealing with Shock and Disbelief

Dealing with early shock and disbelief may be a tough process, but there are practical actions you can take to navigate through these feelings.

Here are some suggestions:

1. Acknowledge your sentiments:

Start by identifying and embracing your sentiments of shock and astonishment. It's common to feel a variety of emotions during stressful circumstances.

2. Give Yourself Time:

Allow yourself the necessary time to comprehend what has transpired. Avoid speeding the healing process, since it is crucial to allow your mind and emotions time to adapt.

3. Seek Support:

Reach out to friends, relatives, or a trusted confidant. Sharing your thoughts and feelings with someone you trust may provide comfort and understanding at this tough time.

4. Professional Help:

Consider obtaining professional treatment from a therapist or counselor. They may provide support, coping skills, and an impartial viewpoint to help you navigate through the shock and disbelief.

5. Self-Care:

Prioritize self-care to guarantee your physical and emotional well-being. Engage in things that provide you comfort and relaxation, such as exercise, meditation, or hobbies.

6. Information Gathering:

Gather facts on the scenario that has produced shock and bewilderment. Understanding the facts may sometimes aid in understanding the reality of the situation.

7. Create a Support System:

Build a support system around you, including friends, family, and community resources. Having a network of people to depend on might make the process more doable.

8. Set realistic expectations:

Understand that healing takes time, and it's normal not to have all the answers immediately. Set reasonable expectations for yourself and allow for incremental growth.

9. Journaling:

Consider maintaining a diary to communicate your ideas and feelings. Writing may be a therapeutic technique to relieve pent-up sentiments and get clarity on your views.

10. Focus on the Present:

Instead of becoming overwhelmed by the past or worrying about the future, try to concentrate on the current moment. Taking tiny steps and tackling one problem at a time might be more achievable.

Remember, everyone copes differently, so it's crucial to identify what works best for you. If your symptoms remain or increase, finding professional treatment is vital for continuous support and direction.

CHAPTER 3

GRIEF AND HEALING

Comprehending the Grief Spectrum

Grief, a common human emotion, takes center stage. The purpose of this chapter is to encourage readers to investigate the complex process of grieving over the loss of a meaningful connection. Grief is a spectrum of feelings that progresses from shock and denial to anger, bargaining, despair, and acceptance. It is not a linear process. People who are aware of this spectrum are better equipped to ride the emotional waves with resilience and self-compassion.

Bereavement is an individualized, diverse, and intricate journey that does not suit one person perfectly. This section of the chapter introduces the idea of a spectrum in an effort to clarify the complexities of mourning.

Grief is no longer seen as a sequential process but rather as a spectrum of emotions that change and grow over time, much like a kaleidoscope of sentiments.

1.   **Shock and Denial:** Shock and denial are common during the early phases of mourning. It's the disorienting sensation of not quite understanding the situation as it really is. This range serves as a defense mechanism, allowing the mind to progressively process the severity of the loss. People may navigate the early phases of mourning with a framework if they recognize that these feelings are a normal reaction.

2.   **Anger and Bargaining:** When the truth sinks in, these are the kinds of feelings that might surface. Anger might be aimed at the cosmos, at oneself, or even at other people. A wish to go back in time and a longing for what was lost are elements of bargaining. Acknowledging and identifying these feelings is essential to moving up the spectrum. Rather than being indicators of weakness, they are essential steps in the healing process.

3.   Depression: Depression is often an indication of a more thorough mourning process. It's a deep heartbreak that shows the weight of the loss and reaches below the surface.

This range of emotions emphasizes how crucial it is to acknowledge that experiencing extreme grief is a normal part of the trip and to give oneself permission to experience it.

4.   Acceptance: Acceptance is at the extreme of the spectrum. It's about learning to live with the loss, not about pushing the hurt away or forgetting it. This region of the spectrum denotes a change from highly charged feelings to a more comprehensive comprehension of the novel situation. Seeking a way to go ahead with the lessons learned from the event is what acceptance entails, not seeking closure.

People may manage these feelings more self-aware if they are aware of the range of sorrow. It serves as a reminder that grieving is a dynamic, ever-evolving process rather than a straight line with a set goal.

This knowledge enables people to accept the complexity of their feelings and offers a path forward for the next chapters, which center on accepting the emotional rollercoaster, resolving guilt and blame, creating a network of support, and engaging in self-compassion exercises as part of the healing process.

Accepting the Emotional Rollercoaster

It's common to compare grief to a rollercoaster because of its erratic highs and lows. Readers are urged to accept the turbulent emotional journey without passing judgment in this part.

All feelings, whether they be grief, rage, or sudden relief, have a place in the healing process. People may process bereavement with a greater awareness of their inner terrain if they give these feelings room.

1. Validating Every Feeling: Grief elicits a spectrum of feelings, just as a rollercoaster includes highs and lows. Emotions such as sadness, rage, perplexity, and relief are all legitimate and need to be acknowledged.

The idea that there is no "right" or "wrong" way to mourn is emphasized in this section. It's about allowing oneself to feel without guilt or pressure to live up to social norms.

2.   Handling Unpredictable Situations: Bereavement is erratic. A surge of strong emotion could sweep over you one day and leave you feeling peaceful the next.

The healing process naturally has these ups and downs. It is suggested that readers approach these situations with inquiry and self-compassion. What sets off certain feelings? How do these feelings change with time? Through impartial observation, people may acquire an understanding of their own process of recovery.

3.   Identifying Unexpected Relief Moments: Despite the depths of loss, there may sometimes be brief bursts of delight or even unexpected relief. This end of the spectrum is as important as times of sadness. It is explained to readers how to identify and value these times, realizing that happiness doesn't take away from the value or love of a relationship that has been lost.

It serves as a reminder that the healing process is complex and non-linear.

4. Developing Presence and Mindfulness: Accepting the rollercoaster calls for developing presence, or a sharpened awareness of the here and now.

With mindfulness, people are able to be completely present with their emotions instead of being overwhelmed by their complexities.

When people are experiencing emotional upheaval, techniques like deep breathing, meditation, or even just being aware of their feelings may help them stay grounded.

5. Journaling as a Reflective Practice: Keeping a journal is an effective way to manage the emotional rollercoaster. Readers are encouraged to write reflectively in this part, sharing their ideas and emotions. A physical record of the emotional journey may be obtained via journaling, which can also shed light on triggers, trends, and resilient moments.

By accepting the emotional rollercoaster, people set out on a path of self-discovery.

It's about establishing an environment where feelings are accepted and included in the healing process, rather than ignored or repressed.

This method encourages self-compassion, resilience, and a better comprehension of the emotional terrain that the mourning process entails.

Getting Over the Pitfalls of Blame and Guilt

Blame and guilt may be very strong roadblocks to recovery. These feelings may obstruct development, whether they are blame for the breakup or remorse over the relationship's termination. This section of the chapter offers strategies for avoiding these traps, encouraging self-forgiveness, and realizing that maintaining partnerships requires cooperation from both parties.

· Recognizing the Sources of Guilt

Guilt is often caused by feelings of accountability for the breakdown of a relationship or for perceived transgressions made during it.

This part acknowledges that relationships are complex and multidimensional and invites readers to investigate the sources of their guilt. It involves redefining self-blame in light of the shared dynamics that aided in the development of the partnership.

· **Challenge Irrational Beliefs**

Irrational expectations or beliefs, such as the idea that one person is exclusively to blame for a relationship's success or failure, may sometimes serve as a source of guilt. This section of the chapter helps readers confront these false assumptions and cultivate a more accurate and balanced understanding of the intricacies of interpersonal relationships.

· **Cultivating Self-Forgiveness**

A transforming part of the healing process is learning to forgive oneself. It entails accepting responsibility for errors made without giving in to an endless blame game. This section offers helpful strategies for developing self-forgiveness while highlighting the fact that mistakes are made by everyone and that progress often results from the lessons discovered during trying circumstances.

· Acknowledging the Role of Blame

Holding oneself or the ex-partner responsible for your problems might prevent you from moving on. This section of the chapter asks readers to identify how blame affects their emotional state. It looks at the notion that assigning blame is often a kind of self-defense, a means to rationalize suffering and regain some measure of control when faced with loss.

· Moving Towards Personal Responsibility

This part helps readers develop a more positive concept of personal responsibility while still recognizing the influence of outside variables on the course of a relationship.

It's important to acknowledge the areas in which one may progress personally rather than take full responsibility. By putting more emphasis on personal accountability than blame, people are better equipped to learn from their mistakes and make wise decisions going forward.

People make room for self-compassion and healing by avoiding the traps of blame and guilt. It's about releasing oneself from the weight of excessive guilt or laying unwarranted blame at the feet of another. Rather, this method facilitates a fair-minded viewpoint that recognizes the mutual aspects of relationships and opens the door to a more compassionate and self-sufficient path toward recovery.

Putting Together a Support Network

Grief's difficulties might be made worse by isolation. Emotional support and useful viewpoints may be obtained from friends, family, or even professional counselors. This section helps readers connect with others, communicate their needs, and create a network that supports their recovery process.

1. Finding Trustworthy Allies: The first step in creating a support network is to find trustworthy allies, or people who can provide a safe environment for discussing feelings and experiences.

Readers are urged to consider their connections and identify individuals who have previously shown empathy and compassion in this section. Friends, relatives, or even coworkers with a caring demeanor may be trusted allies.

2. Expressing Needs and Boundaries: Clear communication is essential for providing effective assistance. It is advised for readers to communicate their demands and limits to others in their support system.

Clear communication creates a supportive atmosphere that is customized to each person's preferences, regardless of the sort of support required, such as a listening ear or practical aid, or the desire for private moments.

3. Professional help: Professional help may play a significant role in the healing process, in addition to personal ties. The concept of consulting therapists, counselors, or support groups is introduced in this section.

These experts may offer an unbiased viewpoint as well as practical skills and coping mechanisms for grieving individuals.

The chapter exhorts readers to perceive obtaining professional assistance as a courageous and self-careful gesture.

4. Building Mutually Beneficial Relationships: Creating a support network requires reciprocity. Exchange-based partnerships, or reciprocal connections, may be very fulfilling. This section of the chapter challenges readers to think about what they can do to improve the health of their support system. Kindness and reciprocity build relationships and provide a supportive atmosphere for one another.

5. Diversifying Your Sources of Assistance: A more extensive network may be established by using a variety of sources of assistance. To provide a well-rounded support system, this section proposes taking into account various connection types, including those with friends, family, coworkers, and support groups. Increasing the diversity of your support network gives you access to a wider variety of viewpoints and emotional support.

6. Using Technology: In the linked world of today, technology may be a useful instrument for creating and sustaining a support network.

This section of the chapter examines how virtual relationships may provide emotional support and act as a bridge over physical boundaries. Examples of these relationships include online support groups and video conversations with loved ones.

Creating a network of support is an acknowledgment of the desire for understanding and connection that all people have, not a show of weakness. In order to build resilience and fortitude to face the difficulties of grieving and healing, this chapter exhorts readers to actively build their support system.

How to Exercise Self-Compassion

Healing begins with self-compassion. Readers are urged by this chapter to treat themselves with the same compassion and consideration that they would provide to a friend who is experiencing hardship. People may change how they relate to sorrow by practicing self-compassion, which will help them see it as a normal part of life rather than a sign of weakness.

1. Suffering Recognition Without Judgment: The first step towards developing self-compassion is to recognize suffering without passing judgment.

The purpose of this section is to help readers understand that mourning is a normal, complicated process and that the feelings one experiences are appropriate reactions to loss. It's about realizing that there is no "right" or "wrong" way to mourn and letting go of self-criticism.

2. Developing a Positive Inner Conversation: During a period of mourning, one may have a strong inner conversation that is full of criticism and self-doubt.

Developing an affirming inner dialogue is a necessary part of practicing self-compassion. The author provides guidance on how to reframe pessimistic thinking and treat oneself with the same kindness and support that they would provide to a friend in the same circumstance. This change in self-talk helps create an emotionally supportive atmosphere.

3.   Accepting Imperfection: Feeling vulnerable and flawed is a common side effect of grief.

This section of the chapter exhorts readers to accept their flaws and weaknesses as essential characteristics of being human. It's about realizing that healing is a slow, non-linear process and letting go of irrational expectations.

4.   Self-Care as a Form of Compassion: Taking care of oneself is a concrete way to show compassion for oneself.

This section examines several types of self-care, such as engaging in physical activity, fostering interests, and taking time for relaxation. Making self-care a priority helps people recognize their health and make room for healing, even in the face of sadness.

5.   Acquiring Knowledge from Failures: Failures are an inherent aspect of the recovery process. Developing self-compassion entails accepting these failures as lessons without passing judgment on oneself. It's about realizing that healing is a series of steps forward and sometimes backward rather than a

straight path and seeing setbacks as chances for growth and insight.

6.   Present-moment awareness and mindfulness: A key component of self-compassion is mindfulness, which is the ability to remain in the present moment without passing judgment. The mindfulness techniques covered in this section of the chapter include deep breathing and meditation. People may manage the intricacies of sorrow with more resilience and self-awareness if they remain rooted in the here and now. Being self-compassionate requires constant tolerance, kindness, and understanding.

Through the application of these concepts to the mourning process, people establish the groundwork for internal healing.

In order to build a loving and supportive connection with themselves while they travel the road of sorrow and healing, this chapter exhorts readers to treat themselves with the same compassion and understanding that they show to others.

The groundwork for a thorough examination of grieving and the process of moving on after a breakup is laid in Chapter 3. It provides useful tools, emotional support, and a caring viewpoint, enabling people to successfully negotiate the range of emotions that surface following sorrow.

CHAPTER 4

SELF-REDISCOVERY

The process of self-discovery entails a deep journey of reflection and self-analysis. In order to comprehend oneself better, it entails exploring one's ideas, feelings, and experiences. Reflection on one's own values, beliefs, and objectives is often necessary for this process.

People may find hidden qualities, pinpoint opportunities for personal development, and clarify their life's purpose through self-discovery. It's an ongoing process that might include accepting change, questioning presumptions, and confronting viewpoints.

In the process of self-rediscovery, techniques like writing, pursuing new experiences, and practicing mindfulness may be very helpful. This transformational process is further facilitated by asking for criticism, having meaningful discussions with people, and being receptive to personal development.

In the end, self-rediscovery is a continuous process that enables people to change, adapt, and live truly—that is, to match their behavior with who they really are.

Accepting Personal Development

The topic of Chapter 4 is coming to terms with who you are after a heartbreak. It highlights the transforming nature of human development and investigates the ways in which people might intentionally and resiliently manage this process.

1. Self-Reflection as a Catalyst: In order to improve personally, self-reflection is a potent catalyst. This section invites readers to reflect on their beliefs, goals, and prior experiences as they set out on a path of self-discovery. It's about getting a clear picture of the person they want to be and who they are right now.

Self-reflection means knowing who you are now and who you want to be in the future, not simply who you were in the past. Allocate a certain period of time for reflection.

Think about your principles, convictions, and the lessons you gained from your previous partnership. Think about your areas of strength and improvement.

What makes you happy? This profound self-awareness serves as the cornerstone of purposeful and significant personal development.

2.   Developing Intentions: Developing intentions is a proactive step in the direction of human development. Readers are assisted in setting clear, attainable objectives for their physical, mental, and emotional health. Whether the goal is to pursue education, take up new activities, or develop closer relationships with loved ones, establishing intentions offers a path forward.

Transforming self-reflection into attainable objectives is the process of setting intentions. Establish clear, attainable goals for all facets of your life, including your physical and mental health, social relationships, intellectual interests, and emotional stability. These objectives act as a road map to help you on your path to self-discovery. They provide you with focus and direction, assisting you in directing your efforts into areas that support your goals.

3.   New Interests and Passions: A key component of self-discovery is investigating new interests and passions.

This section of the chapter explores the value of broadening one's interests, whether they be in the form of academic, physical, or artistic undertakings.

Taking part in happy and fulfilling activities helps foster a sense of self that exists independently of the past relationship.

Traveling to unknown places is frequently a necessary part of self-discovery. Take part in things that make you happy and pique your interest. Experiencing new things, rekindling old passions, or exploring uncharted hobbies are all examples of how this book enhances one's sense of self. It's a chance to reinvent yourself outside of the parameters of your last partnership.

4.   Building a good attitude: Personal development is based on having a good attitude. This section looks at techniques for developing optimism, such as affirmations, gratitude journals, and rephrasing unfavorable ideas. People become more resilient and receptive to new opportunities when they cultivate a cheerful outlook.

An optimistic outlook is a powerful friend on the path to self-discovery. This is a conscious activity that entails more than merely thinking positively. Recognize the blessings in your life and practice appreciation. Add inspiring and motivating affirmations. Recalibrate your negative thinking to see obstacles as chances for personal development. Positivity broadens your horizons and allows you to see opportunities.

5. Developing Emotional Resilience: Regaining one's emotional resilience is essential to self-discovery. This section of the chapter offers strategies for developing emotional resilience, such as accepting vulnerability, practicing emotional control, and engaging in mindfulness. Building resilience gives people the capacity to handle adversity gracefully and adaptably.

Resilience in the face of adversity is a sign of emotional resilience. Examine mindfulness techniques to help you remain rooted in the here and now, such as deep breathing and meditation. Acquire efficient emotional regulation skills. Accept your vulnerability as a strength instead of a weakness. Developing emotional resilience gives you the capacity to handle life's inevitable ups and downs with grace and flexibility.

6. Building Healthy Connections: The chapter addresses the significance of building healthy connections as people come to terms with who they are again. Developing strong relationships—whether via reestablishing old ties or making new ones—contributes to a network of support that fosters personal development.

The path of rediscovery is not an isolated one. It entails building new, wholesome connections as well as reestablishing old ones. Embrace a community of people who encourage and support you.

Cultivate connections that enhance your overall health. Setting boundaries with unhealthy relationships and actively fostering connections that support your development may be necessary to achieve this.

7. The Function of Gratitude in Healing: During the process of self-discovery, gratitude has a transformational role. This section looks at how practicing thankfulness may improve wellbeing, cause perspective shifts, and provide the groundwork for personal development. Resilience and abundance are fostered by recognizing and enjoying life's good parts.

Gratitude is a transforming energy that helps you concentrate on the abundance in your life rather than the things that are missing. Develop an attitude of thankfulness every day.

Give yourself time to enjoy the little things in life. Gratitude becomes a compass, forming a way of thinking that supports your recovery and allows you to proceed with a feeling of plenty and richness.

Readers are walked through the process of finding themselves again after grief in Chapter 4. It gives people activities, a caring viewpoint, and useful insights that enable them to embrace personal development on their journey toward a revitalized sense of self.

Forgiveness and Moving On

Following a breakup, the road to recovery often passes through the territory of forgiveness and the transforming act of letting go. This chapter serves as a compass, helping people navigate the complex process of accepting forgiveness, seeing the value of letting go for their own wellbeing, and embracing the wide range of new options.

1.   Understanding Forgiveness

The Alchemy of Release:

A powerful alchemy that turns suffering into release is forgiveness.

This section explores the complex concept of forgiveness, highlighting that it is a significant release from the emotional bonds that bind the heart rather than a condonation of behavior. Recognizing forgiveness's ability to release people from the weight of bitterness and rage and give them back control over their emotional environments is essential to understanding it.

The Path to Compassion:

Empathy, or the capacity to see the humanity in both oneself and the one who injured you, is often linked to forgiveness. This section of the chapter delves into the pathway that leads from forgiveness to compassion, as people see the common vulnerabilities that allow them to go beyond the roles of perpetrator and victim.

2. Letting Go to Ensure Your Health

The Burden of Emotional Attachments:

The lingering effects of emotional baggage make sorrow seem more permanent. This section explains the importance of letting go—not as a forgetful act, but as a deliberate choice to let go of the things that impede personal development. A key component of self-care is letting go, which enables people to move into the healing and well-being light.

Accepting Emotional Autonomy:

Regaining emotional freedom involves letting go. It entails letting go of the wounds from the past, clearing the heart, and giving oneself permission to go forward. This section of the chapter highlights the relationship between wellbeing and letting go, showing how consciously releasing emotional attachments may act as a trigger for recovery and rejuvenation.

3.   Experiencing Unexpected Opportunities

Accepting the White Space:

New possibilities appear like a blank canvas ready to be painted as forgiveness and letting go make room in the heart. The idea of emotional liberation—the ability to rethink one's life, relationships, and personal goals—is examined in this section. Allowing oneself to be open to new possibilities invites one to go into unknown areas and find the delight of self-discovery.

Building up resilience:

Moving forward is a sign of resiliency rather than a rejection of the past.

This section of the chapter sheds light on the relationship that exists between resilience building, letting go, and forgiving. It explores how these life-changing experiences strengthen people and provide them with the ability to face problems in the future with a fresh sense of self-awareness and strength.

This chapter is essentially an empowerment story, a manual for the difficult process of forgiving and letting go.

It honors the human spirit's tenacity by demonstrating how, via these transforming deeds, people not only overcome grief but also become receptive to the limitless possibilities of fresh starts.

Reconnecting with Joy

Recovering from heartbreak is more than simply getting well; it's about finding happiness again and starting over with a life full of passion, supportive relationships, and the thrilling embrace of fresh beginnings. This chapter acts as a compass, pointing people in the direction of a fulfilling path toward finding pleasure again.

Finding New Interests and Passions:

Using Passion as a Remedy:

Exploring passions and interests is frequently the first step towards rediscovering pleasure.

The transforming potential of participating in activities that spark passion and creativity is discussed in this section. Taking up a long-lost interest or exploring new ground, this trip becomes a means of self-discovery and reestablishing a connection with the pleasure that is ingrained in one's hobbies.

Developing Flow States:

Enthusiastic endeavors often result in the sensation of "flow," a condition in which people are totally absorbed in what they are doing, losing track of time and overcoming the limitations of the outside world. This section of the chapter explores the practice of creating flow states as a way to rekindle pleasure. It explores how these engrossing moments turn into a haven of recovery and renewal.

Fostering Harmonious Connections

Developing Cordial Relationships:

Good connections serve as moorings for the journey back to happiness. The significance of building supportive and uplifting relationships is emphasized in this section. Positive interactions are essential for creating a joyful atmosphere and for strengthening current friendships as well as establishing new ones.

Laughter and experiences shared:

In the context of healthy relationships, laughter turns into a therapeutic salve. Genuine laughter, joyful moments, and shared experiences weave a tapestry of pleasure that shines through the shadows of sadness. In this section of the chapter, the mechanics of shared pleasure are examined, showing how wholesome relationships may serve as pathways to recovery and self-discovery.

· **Opening a Fresh Chapter**

The Void Space of Prospect:

Opening a new chapter is a statement of hope and a monument to resilience. This section encourages people to think of their lives as empty canvases that may be filled with the hues of fresh possibilities and experiences. It's an investigation of the liberation that results from moving on from the past and into the unexplored regions of an unwritten future that is just waiting to be revealed.

Having Joyful Intentions:

The path to rediscovering pleasure adopts intentionality as a guiding concept. This section of the chapter encourages people to make joyful choices by figuring out what makes them happy, actively looking for good things to happen to them, and making joy the main character in their life stories.

This chapter is essentially a celebration of the human spirit's innate resilience. It highlights the transforming power of happiness and shows that there is always a dawn to be welcomed, even after the darkest hours of sorrow.

Regaining joy becomes a journey of self-discovery, satisfaction, and rediscovering the innate beauty of life rather than a goal.

Readers are guided to actively create a future consistent with their enhanced self-awareness. It gives people exercises, a compassionate viewpoint, and useful insights that enable them to set out on a meaningful path with resilience and intentionality.

Healing Together

"Healing Together" explores the delicate dance that happens as people try to heal the wounds that tragedy has inflicted, both within themselves and in the common areas of relationships. This chapter leads the group through the process of healing together, guiding them through the difficult process of mending relationships, talking things out to gain closure, and realizing that forgiveness is a two-way street.

1.   Mending Broken Bonds

The Craft of Reconstruction:

Reconstruction, the fine art of repairing relationships after tragedy, is necessary.

This section explores the intricate process of mending stressed or broken relationships. It entails a common goal for a restored relationship as well as a commitment to empathy and understanding on both sides. The chapter examines doable tactics for overcoming the difficulties involved in mending relationships, with a strong emphasis on perseverance, attentive listening, and a sincere desire to work together toward healing.

Establishing Healthy Boundaries:

Establishing sound limits becomes essential when connections are rebuilt. This section of the chapter delves into the significance of setting up boundaries that are considerate and unambiguous in order to safeguard the welfare of all parties concerned. It's an exploration of how to create an atmosphere that allows both people to recover and flourish while striking a balance between intimacy and independence.

2.   Bringing Things to a Close

Honest Talks:

Good communication turns into a link to resolution. This section highlights the importance of having open and honest talks where people feel free to share their thoughts, emotions, and opinions. Establishing a secure environment for conversation where all parties feel heard and understood is essential to communicating for closure. It's an investigation of how words may help people resolve their emotions and open the door to one another's recovery.

Recognizing Problems:

It is often necessary to acknowledge problems and unsolved difficulties in order to get closure. This section of the chapter pushes people to face their discomfort in order to create a space where tough talks may result in understanding and, eventually, closure. It's an understanding that going ahead with a fresh perspective requires an honest assessment of the past as well as a commitment to mending together.

3.   The Two-Way Street of Forgiveness:

Mutual Acts of Pardoning:

It takes two to forgive; forgiveness is not a one-way transaction. This section explores the concept of reciprocity in forgiveness, when both parties recognize and accept responsibility for their respective contributions to the healing process. It examines how mutual actions of forgiveness provide the groundwork for restoring confidence and fostering a fresh bond.

The Potential for Change in Mutual Forgiveness:

When forgiveness is reciprocated, it has transformational power. This section of the chapter demonstrates how people are united in their common commitment to healing through the act of forgiving and receiving forgiveness.

It entails letting go of grudges, cultivating empathy, and welcoming the possibility of a future characterized by understanding and progress for everyone.

"Healing Together" is essentially a recognition that the road to recovery is longer than just one person's rehabilitation; it entails working together to mend relationships, communicating openly in order to find closure, and seeing forgiveness as a shared journey. This chapter serves as a guide for those negotiating the complex landscape of collaborative healing, providing perspectives and tactics to encourage a path towards restored relationships and group health.

Formulating a Future Vision

Building a future with purpose is the main topic of Chapter 5, which emphasizes the significance of imagining a life that is in line with your newly discovered self-discovery. It walks readers through the process of formulating a future vision that aligns with their beliefs, interests, and goals.

1. Determining Your Personal Values: Knowing your basic principles is the first step towards building a meaningful future. Readers are asked to define and explain their own values in this part. Which values have the most significance for you? In what ways do these ideals influence your choices and behavior?

Making sense of one's own values might serve as a compass for directing one's destiny toward what is most important.

 2. Establishing Long-Term Goals: Creating a purposeful future requires establishing long-term objectives that align with your dreams. This section of the chapter challenges readers to look beyond their current problems and take the big picture into consideration.

What experiences and successes do you want to have over the next five, 10, or twenty years? Establishing long-term objectives helps build a route map for the future.

3. Accepting Adaptability and Flexibility: Accepting flexibility is just as important as having objectives. Because life is unpredictable, things might change. The significance of continuing to be flexible and receptive to new opportunities is discussed in this section.

It promotes resilience in the face of unforeseen difficulties by encouraging readers to see diversions as chances for learning and personal development.

4. Developing a Growth Mindset: A growth mindset is an effective way of thinking that sees obstacles as chances for personal progress. This section of the chapter explores the development of a growth mindset. How do you handle challenges and setbacks? People who embrace learning and ongoing development may construct a resilient future by navigating the challenges of creating a meaningful future.

5. A meaningful future requires careful planning that takes into account striking a balance between immediate satisfaction and long-term goals. This section looks at how to balance your short-term needs with your long-term objectives. It's about striking a balance that is consistent with your ideals and making decisions that advance both your current and future sense of satisfaction.

6. Developing Self-Compassion in the Process: Self-compassion is necessary on the path to a meaningful future.

This section of the chapter highlights how crucial it is to treat oneself with kindness while negotiating the unknowns of the future. It's about realizing that errors and diversions are a necessary component of development and education. Positivity and resilience are fostered by practicing self-compassion.

7. Honoring Significant Achievers: Creating a meaningful future involves a number of actions and turning points. The purpose of this section is to inspire readers to recognize and appreciate their modest victories along the journey. Acknowledging progress encourages people to keep working toward their long-term goals and adds to their feeling of success.

CHAPTER 5:

CONCLUSION

The finish acts as the crescendo in the healing symphony, inviting reflection on the path that has transformed and acceptance of the possibilities that lie ahead. This last chapter tackles the concepts of accepting a new self and going ahead with fortitude. It is full of depth and relevance. The story of grief is brought to a close as the curtain rises to show a stage painted in the hues of resiliency, self-discovery, and the hope for a better, more powerful future.

Embracing a Renewed Self

The Renewal Tapestry:

It's important to be amazed by the complexity of self-renewal as we approach the end. This section honors the fabric of rebirth that people create as they go through the phases of recovery.

It is evidence of the resiliency that permits the formation of a new self, molded by self-reflection, genuineness, and the bravery to face hardship.

Honoring Personal Development:

Accepting your transformed self is a recognition of your own development. This section of the epilogue delves into the metamorphosis that takes place when people face sorrow, negotiate the challenges of recovery, and come out on the other side with an enhanced sense of self-awareness. It's a celebration of the lessons learned, the vulnerabilities accepted, and the strengths unearthed throughout the healing process.

The Internal Phoenix:

Every heart that has survived tragedy harbors a phoenix, a symbol of resiliency that emerges from the ashes of suffering. This part explores the meaning of the internal phoenix, showing how the healing process turns people into strong, resilient beings who can overcome the most trying situations.

The Revealing of Genuineness:

Revealing oneself requires exposing one's true nature. This section of the chapter delves into the emancipation that arises from removing the masks of society and discovering one's genuine self. It's a tribute to the freedom that comes with accepting one's own path, the beauty found in sincerity, and the bravery found in vulnerability.

Pressing Forward with Power

The Forward Momentum's Power:

The idea of forging ahead with power becomes more important as the story progresses toward its climax. The transforming power of forward momentum—a dynamic force that lifts people out of the shadows of the past and into the bright possibilities of the future—is examined in this section.

Using Your Resilience:

Using the resilience that has been developed throughout the healing chapters is essential to going ahead with strength.

This section of the conclusion explores the ways in which resilience turns into a compass that helps people find their way through life's uncertainties. It's an investigation of the resilience that comes from realizing that one can go on with strength even in the face of scars.

The Embroidery of Fresh Starts:

Every ending signifies the start of a new chapter. This section asks readers to see the tapestry of fresh starts as a blank canvas ready to be painted with the hues of pleasure, goals, and self-discovery. It's an investigation of the possibilities and thrills that come with forging forward and welcoming the unknown with an adventurous and self-empowering mindset.

The Empowerment Echo:

Proceeding with courage is a declaration of empowerment, a thundering confirmation of the inner fortitude that turns misfortune into opportunity. This section of the conclusion celebrates resilience's ability to empower, the bravery to let go of the past, and the acceptance of a future in which strength serves as a guiding companion.

Finishing the Section, Begins the Novel:

Let the last pages of this book serve as a transition rather than a point of conclusion—a new chapter beginning and a new chapter finishing. The process of getting over a breakup is not a straight line; rather, it's a complex, dynamic story with many turns and significant epiphanies.

I hope the lessons learned inside these pages find resonance in the echoes of daily existence. May the tales of self-revelation, group healing, and the joyous rebirth of self-function serve as compass points in the night sky of personal development. As you flip the last page, keep in mind that every ending serves as a bridge to a fresh start. Welcome the new you with open arms, go forward with the power you've gained from the healing crucible, and may the next chapter be a symphony of happiness, self-awareness, and the many opportunities that lie ahead.

www.ingramcontent.com/pod-product-compliance
Lightning Source LLC
Chambersburg PA
CBHW060956260726
48661CB00005B/1901